P9-DMC-776

A Guide for the Advanced Soul

A BOOK OF INSIGHT

HOW TO USE THIS GUIDE

You have a problem or need guidance to help you make a decision. Picture this clearly in your mind; meditate on it so that the mind gradually subsides into stillness. This allows you to draw on your subconscious and intuitive powers to respond.

Now put forward your request while randomly opening the book. The first words you read will tell you what you most need to hear.

Clearly it is your interpretation of the saying that will give you your answer. Be open to what you read; interpreting it objectively, without projecting your wishes on the outcome. The value of the reading will depend on how far you are willing to change in the direction indicated. Opposing the forces controlling your life creates your disharmony.

Knowing that you create your personal reality is most important because then you understand that all exterior circumstances, events and experiences in the world flow from the centre of your being to provide a living feedback.

What is written in this book will tell you everything you need to know. At this instant you are a reflection of the universe where all things and events exist simultaneously — the past, present and the future juxtaposed — and you contain all the potentialities of the whole world within you.

Your guidance is here for you to work from the point of your own reality.

A Guide for the Advanced Soul

A BOOK OF INSIGHT

Created & Handwritten by

SUSAN HAYWARD

IN · TUNE BOOKS

IN-TUNE BOOKS
PO BOX 1093
CROWS NEST NSW 2065
AUSTRALIA

First Published in February 1985
Revised Edition December 1986
This Reprint April 1990

A GUIDE FOR THE ADVANCED SOUL

Jacket Calligraphy by Margo Snape
Illustrations by Shane McCoy

Produced by Mandarin Offset, HK.

ISBN 0-9590439-O-X

By the same author
BEGIN IT NOW   ISBN 0-9590439-1-8 *1987*
BAG OF JEWELS   ISBN 0-9590439-2-6 *1988*

International Distributors:

AUST	Collins Angus & Robertson, Sydney
NZ	Lothian Books, Auckland
USA	Bookpeople SF, New Leaf GA, DeVorss LA, Inland CT

A Letter to You

Dear Friend :

I have created this book for you to consult when you are faced with problems. It is a collection of beautiful words of wisdom that will guide and inspire you.

See yourself as part of the never-ending cycle of change in the universe and this book will reflect that change for you. Everything in the universe is continuously integrating and disintegrating- this produces transformation and growth. Your problems are caused by your resistance towards this natural cyclic movement of life.

When you randomly open this Guide you are addressing the universe, and it responds to your question, which you then interpret intuitively. Regard your problems as opportunities for learning and creating something new, and you will feel a sense of well-being that results from your shift in consciousness. Know that we are only presented with lessons when we are ready to learn them.

Above all, trust your own direction. I hope this Guide gives you confidence to follow your path and surrender to the inner intuitive voice that recognises the harmony and wholeness that has always been there.

I hope also that this contributes to the increasing new awareness and social transformation taking place throughout the world, that will unite all human beings as One.

Love,
Susan

Life is the movie
    you see
        through your own,
            unique eyes.

It makes little difference
    what's happening out there.

    It's how you take it that counts.

DENIS WAITLEY
The Winner's Edge

Set your sights high,
   the higher the better.

Expect the most wonderful things
   to happen, not in the future
   but right now.

Realise that nothing is too good.

Allow absolutely nothing
   to hamper you
   or hold you up
   in any way.

EILEEN CADDY
Footprints on the Path

To see your drama
            clearly
is to be liberated
        from it.

KEN KEYES, JR
Handbook to Higher Consciousness

*A human being
is a single being.*

*Unique
and unrepeatable.*

JOHN PAUL II

Have no fear
   of moving into the unknown.
Simply step out fearlessly
   knowing that I am with you,
   therefore no harm can befall you;
   all is very very well.

Do this in complete faith
   and confidence.

EILEEN CADDY
Footprints on the Path

Life is a series
    of natural
        and spontaneous
            changes.

Don't resist them -
            that only creates sorrow.

    Let reality be reality.

Let things flow naturally forward
    in whatever way
        they like.

LAO-TSE

Experience
is determined by yourself -

not the circumstances
of your life.

GITA BELLIN

When you feel
　　that you have reached the end
and that you cannot go
　　　　　one step further,
when life seems to be
　　drained of all purpose:

What a wonderful opportunity
　to start all over again,
　　to turn over a new page.

EILEEN CADDY
Footprints on the Path

To find yourself,
Think for yourself.

SOCRATES

A tree that can fill the span
    of a man's arms
    grows from a downy tip;

A terrace nine storeys high
    rises from hodfuls of earth;

A journey of a thousand miles
    starts from beneath one's feet.

LAO-TZU

Stride forward
   with a firm, steady step
   knowing with
      a deep, certain
         inner knowing
   that you will reach
   every goal you set yourselves,
   that you will achieve
         every aim.

EILEEN CADDY
Footprints on the Path

When you affirm your own
rightness in the universe,
then you co-operate with others easily
and automatically
as part of your own nature.

You, being yourself,
help others
be themselves.

Because you recognise
your own uniqueness
you will not need
to dominate others,
nor cringe before them.

JANE ROBERTS
The Nature of Personal Reality

Inner peace
can be reached
only when we practice
forgiveness.

Forgiveness
is the letting go of the past,
and is therefore
the means for correcting
our misperceptions.

GERALD G. JAMPOLSKY
Love is Letting Go of Fear

Never be afraid
to tread the path alone.

Know which is your path
and follow it wherever
it may lead you;

do not feel you have to follow
in someone else's
footsteps.

EILEEN CADDY
Footprints on the Path

The impossible is possible
when people align with you.

When you do things with people,
not against them,
the amazing resources
of the Higher Self within
are mobilised.

GITA BELLIN

Be open to your
happiness
and sadness
as they arise.

JOHN & LYN ST. CLAIR THOMAS
Eyes of the Beholder

Live
and work
but do not forget to play,
to have fun in life
and really enjoy it.

EILEEN CADDY
The Dawn of Change

Love alone can unite living beings
so as to complete and fulfill them...
for it alone joins them
by what is deepest
in themselves.

All we need is to imagine
our ability to love developing
until it embraces
the totality of men
and of the earth.

TEILHARD DE CHARDIN

However many holy words
        you read,
however many you speak,
What good will they do you
    if you do not act upon them?

THE DHAMMAPADA

7.

Dwell not on the past.
Use it to illustrate a point,
then leave it behind.
Nothing really matters
except what you do now
in this instant of time.

From this moment onward
you can be an entirely different person,
filled with love and understanding,
ready with an outstretched hand,
uplifted and positive
in every thought
and deed.

EILEEN CADDY
God Spoke to Me

Until one is committed, there is hesitancy, the chance to draw back, always ineffectiveness. Concerning all acts of initiative (and creation), there is one elementary truth, the ignorance of which kills countless ideas and splendid plans: that the moment one definitely commits oneself, then Providence moves too.

All sorts of things occur to help one that would never otherwise have occurred. A whole stream of events issues from the decision, raising in one's favour all manner of unforeseen incidents and meetings and material assistance, which no man could have dreamed would have come his way.

SCOTTISH HIMALAYAN
EXPEDITION

Whatever you can do
or dream you can,
begin it.

Boldness has genius, magic
and power in it.

Begin it now.

GOETHE

All we
see or
seem
is but a dream
within
a
dream.

EDGAR ALLEN POE

Yesterday
    is but today's memory
        and
Tomorrow
    is today's dream.

KAHLIL GIBRAN
The Prophet

We are what we think.
All that we are
    arises with our thoughts.
With our thoughts we make
    the world.

Speak or act with a pure mind
    and happiness will follow you
    as your shadow,
    unshakeable.

THE DHAMMAPADA

A soul without
a high aim
is like a ship
without a rudder.

EILEEN CADDY
The Dawn of Change

It is good to have an end
to journey towards,
but it is the journey that matters,
in the end.

URSULA LE GUIN
The Left Hand of Darkness

Cease trying
    to work everything out
        with your minds.
            it will get you nowhere.

Live by intuition
    and inspiration
        and let your whole life
            be a Revelation.

EILEEN CADDY
Footprints on the Path

The fates lead
   him who will–

   him who won't,
      they drag.

SENECA

Confine yourself
to
the
present.

MARCUS AURELIUS

Seek always
for the answer within.

Be not influenced
by those around you,
by their thoughts
or their words.

EILEEN CADDY
God Spoke to Me

)(

Man cannot discover new oceans
until he has courage
to lose sight
of the shore.

UNKNOWN

I do not expect anything
from others,
So their actions
cannot be in opposition
to wishes of mine.

SWAMI SRI YUKTESWAR
Autobiography of a Yogi

Your questions
indicate the depth
of your belief.

Look at the depth
of your questions.

JOHN & LYN ST. CLAIR THOMAS
Eyes of the Beholder

The secret of making
   something work in your lives is,
first of all,
      the deep desire to make it work:

then the faith and belief
   that it can work:

then to hold that clear definite
vision in your consciousness
and see it working out
   step by step,
      without one thought
         of doubt or disbelief.

EILEEN CADDY
Footprints on the Path

Life is full
and overflowing
with the new.

But it is necessary to empty out
the old to make room
for the new to enter.

EILEEN CADDY
Footprints on the Path

Only in relationship can you know yourself, not in abstraction and certainly not in isolation.

The movement of behaviour is the sure guide to yourself, it's the mirror of your consciousness; this mirror will reveal its content, the images, the attachments, the fears, the loneliness, the joy and sorrow.

Poverty lies in running away from this, either in its sublimations or its identities.

J. KRISHNAMURTI

You make
yourself and
others suffer
just as much
when

you take offense

as when
you give offense.

KEN KEYES, JR
Handbook to Higher Consciousness

The more you depend
on forces
outside yourself,
the more you are dominated
by them.

HAROLD SHERMAN

The most effective way
to achieve right relations
with any living thing
is to look for the best in it,
and then help that best
into the fullest expression.

J. ALLEN BOONE
Kinship with All Life

Let there be more
joy and laughter
in your living.

EILEEN CADDY
God Spoke to Me

Thoughts are things;
    they have tremendous power.

Thoughts of doubt and fear are pathways
    to failure.
When you conquer negative attitudes
    of doubt and fear you conquer failure.

Thoughts crystallize into habit
    and habit solidifies into circumstances.

BRIAN ADAMS
How To Succeed

You are given the gifts of the gods;
  you create your reality
  according to your beliefs.

Yours is the creative energy
  that makes your world.

There are no limitations
  to the self
  except those you believe in.

JANE ROBERTS
The Nature of Personal Reality

A thing is complete
when you can
let it
be.

GITA BELLIN

There is only one courage
and that is the courage
to go on dying to the past,
not to collect it,
not to accumulate it,
not to cling to it.

We all cling to the past,
and because we cling
to the past we become
unavailable
to the present.

BHAGWAN SHREE RAJNEESH
Walking in Zen, Sitting in Zen

The past
  is dead

The future
  is imaginary

Happiness
  can only be

in the Eternal

  Now

  Moment

KEN KEYES, JR
Handbook to Higher Consciousness

One cannot conquer the evil in
himself by resisting it...
but by transmuting its energies
into other forms.

The energy that expresses
itself in the form of evil
is the same energy
which expresses itself
in the form of good;
and thus the one may
be transmuted into the other.

CHARLES HENRY MACKINTOSH
I Looked on Life

Be afraid of nothing
you have within you—
all wisdom
all power
all strength
all understanding.

EILEEN CADDY
The Dawn of Change

If you know
you want it,
Have it.

GITA BELLIN

Expect your every need
to be met,
expect the answer
to every problem,
expect abundance
on every level,
expect to grow spiritually.

EILEEN CADDY
The Dawn of Change

Ask, and it shall be given you;
 seek, and ye shall find;
  knock, and it shall be opened
              unto you.

For every one that asketh,
              receiveth;
and he that seeketh,
              findeth;
and to him that knocketh
 it shall be opened.

MATTHEW 7:7,8

At any moment
I could start being a
better person -

but which moment
should I choose ?

ASHLEIGH BRILLIANT
Potshots No. 1521

One has just to be oneself.
That's my basic message.

The moment you accept yourself
as you are,
all burdens,
all mountainous burdens
simply disappear.

Then life is a sheer joy,
a festival of lights.

BHAGWAN SHREE RAJNEESH
The Sound of One Hand Clapping

When you are inspired by some great
purpose, some extraordinary project,
all your thoughts break their bonds;
Your mind transcends limitations,
your consciousness expands in every direction,
and you find yourself in a new, great
and wonderful world.
Dormant forces, faculties and talents
become alive, and you discover yourself
to be a greater person by far
than you ever dreamed
yourself to be.

PATANJALI

'For those who believe,
 no proof is necessary.

'For those who don't believe,
 no proof is possible.

JOHN & LYN ST. CLAIR THOMAS
Eyes of the Beholder

Take the good until you find something better, and in search for something better do not let the good slip away from you or die out. If you disregard it despite its worth, and pursue something better, what you had escapes you; but if you remain attached to what is good, you will always have it if nothing better follows.

PARACELSUS

We learn wisdom from failure
much more than from success;
We often discover what will do,
by finding out what will not do;
and probably he who never made a mistake
never made a discovery.

SAMUEL SMILES

Like attracts like.

Whatever the conscious mind
thinks and believes,
the subconscious
identically
creates.

BRIAN ADAMS
How To Succeed

The course of human life is like that of a great river which, by the force of its own swiftness, takes quite new and unforeseen channels where before there was no current— such varied currents and unpremeditated changes are part of God's purpose for our lives.

Life is not an artificial canal to be confined within prescribed channels.

When once this is clearly seen in our own lives, then we shall not be able to be misled by any mere fabrications.

RABINDRANATH TAGORE

Be at peace
and see
a clear pattern and plan
running through
all your lives.

Nothing is by chance.

EILEEN CADDY
Footprints on the Path

When love beckons to you, follow him,
Though his ways are hard and steep.
And when his wings enfold you,
yield to him,
Though the sword hidden
among his pinions may wound you.

And when he speaks to you,
believe in him,
Though his voice may shatter your dreams
as the north wind
lays waste the garden.

KAHLIL GIBRAN
The Prophet

Life is either
a daring adventure
or nothing.

HELEN KELLER

There is no situation that could
ever confront you
that cannot be solved.
Life takes on real meaning
when you set values
for yourself,
regard yourself as worthwhile
and elevate your thoughts
to things that are of God-good.
There is a Higher Power.
Turn to it and use it;
It is yours for the asking.

BRIAN ADAMS
How To Succeed

Trials are but lessons
that you failed to learn
presented once again,
so where you made a faulty choice before
you can now make a better one,
and thus escape all pain
that what you chose before
has brought to you.

A COURSE IN MIRACLES

To every thing
there is a season,
and a time to every purpose
under the heaven.

ECCLESIASTES 3:1

Everything
we do in life...

Is it not just a game ?

GURURAJ ANANDA YOGI

Every now and then go away,
 have a little relaxation,
 for when you come back
 to your work
 your judgement will be surer;
 since to remain constantly at work
 will cause you to lose power
                of judgement ...

Go some distance away
 because the work appears smaller
 and more of it
 can be taken in at a glance,
 and a lack of harmony
 or proportion
                is more readily seen.

LEONARDO DA VINCI

Change
is never a loss -

it is change only.

VERNON HOWARD
The Mystic Path to Cosmic Power

If you would learn
the secret
of right relations
look only for the divine
in people and things,
and leave all the rest to God.

J. ALLEN BOONE
Kinship with all Life

We can only
Be Here Now
when we accept instantly
our moment-by-moment
emotional experience.

GITA BELLIN

The greater
    the emphasis
        upon perfection
    the further it recedes.

HARIDAS CHAUDHURI
Mastering the Problems of Living

That which oppresses me,
  is it my soul
  trying to come
  out in the open,
or the soul of the world
knocking at my heart
for its entrance ?

RABINDRANATH TAGORE

Why destroy
   your present happiness
      by a distant misery,
      which may never
      come at all?

For every substantial grief
has twenty shadows
   and most of the shadows
   are of your own making.

SYDNEY SMITH

You find true joy
   and happiness in life
when you give
   and give
      and go on giving
         and never count the cost.

EILEEN CADDY
The Dawn of Change

Success is a journey
not a destination –
half the fun is getting there.

GITA BELLIN

My life is a performance
for which
I was never given
any chance to rehearse.

ASHLEIGH BRILLIANT
Potshots No. 1318

Just look next time you are having some trip and riding a problem - just watch. Just stand aside and look at the problem. Is it really there? Or have you created it?

Look deeply into it, and you will suddenly see it is not increasing, it is decreasing; it is becoming smaller and smaller.

The more you put your energy into observation, the smaller it becomes. And a moment comes when suddenly it is not there... you will have a good laugh.

BHAGWAN SHREE RAJNEESH
The Tantra Vision Vol I

Great spirits
  have always encountered
    violent opposition
      from mediocre minds.

ALBERT EINSTEIN

Forgiveness recognises
what you thought
your brother did to you
has not occurred.

A COURSE IN MIRACLES

Learn to be silent.

Let your
  quiet mind
    listen
      and absorb.

PYTHAGORUS

Every issue,
belief,
attitude
or assumption
is precisely the issue
that stands between
you and your relationship
to another human being;
and between you
and yourself.

GITA BELLIN

Perfect kindness
acts
without thinking
of kindness.

LAO-TSE

Time is an invention.
Now is a reality.
So much creativity is happening
for the simple reason that we
have withdrawn ourselves
from past and future.

Our whole energy remains blocked
either in the past or in the future.

When you withdraw all your energy
from past and future a
tremendous explosion happens.

That explosion is creativity.

BHAGWAN SHREE RAJNEESH
The Goose Is Out

Of a certainty
the man who can see
all creatures in himself,
himself in all creatures,
knows no sorrow.

EESHA UPANISHAD

Every moment of your life
is infinitely creative
and the universe
is endlessly bountiful.

Just put forth
a clear enough request,
and everything
your heart desires
must come to you.

SHAKTI GAWAIN
Creative Visualisation

'Expand
in consciousness –
be ready to accept anything
now,
at any time.

EILEEN CADDY
God Spoke to Me

What we are today
   comes from
   our thoughts of yesterday,
   and our present thoughts
   build our life
   of tomorrow:

Our life is the creation of our mind.

THE BUDDHA

Love is

letting go

of fear.

GERALD JAMPOLSKY

When some misfortune threatens, consider seriously and deliberately what is the very worst that could possibly happen. Having looked this possible misfortune in the face, give yourself sound reasons for thinking that after all it would be no such terrible disaster. Such reasons always exist, since at the worst nothing that happens to oneself has any cosmic importance. When you have looked for some time steadily at the worst possibility and have said to yourself with real conviction, 'Well, after all, that would not matter so very much', you will find that your worry diminishes to a quite extraordinary extent. It may be necessary to repeat the process a few times, but in the end, if you have shirked nothing in facing the worst possible issue, you will find that your worry disappears altogether and is replaced by a kind of exhilaration.

BERTRAND RUSSELL
The Conquest of Happiness

How much longer will you go on
    letting your energy sleep?

How much longer are you going
    to stay oblivious of the immensity
    of yourself?

Don't lose time in conflict;
    lose no time in doubt –
    time can never be recovered
    and if you miss an opportunity
    it may take many lives
    before another comes
    your way again.

BHAGWAN SHREE RAJNEESH
A Cup Of Tea

If you attack apparent negativity
with negativity,
you merely feed
and inflame the source.

It's always best
to take the positive
in any conflict.

If you genuinely love,
or at least
send kind thoughts
to a thing,
it will change
before your eyes.

JOHN & LYN ST. CLAIR THOMAS
Eyes of the Beholder

Everything
I do and say
with anyone
makes a difference.

GITA BELLIN

Difficulties are opportunities
to better things;
they are stepping stones to greater experience.

Perhaps someday you will be thankful
for some temporary failure
in a particular direction.

When one door closes, another always opens;
as a natural law it has to,
to balance.

BRIAN ADAMS
How To Succeed

If you're into guilt
you're playing God.
The universe is created
so it's O.K. to make a mistake.

If you feel guilty about
what you have done,
you're saying
it's not O.K.
to make mistakes.

To change one's life:

· Start immediately

· Do it flamboyantly

· No exceptions (no excuses)

WILLIAM JAMES

By going along with feelings,
  you unify
    your emotional,
      mental,
        and bodily states.

When you try to fight
  or deny them,
you divorce yourself
from the reality of your being.

JANE ROBERTS
The Nature of Personal Reality

To be
upset
over what
you don't have...

is
to waste
what
you do have.

KEN KEYES, JR.
Handbook to Higher Consciousness

Do the thing
and you will
have the Power.

RALPH WALDO EMERSON

The people
we are in relationship
with are always a mirror,
reflecting our own beliefs,
and simultaneously
we are mirrors,
reflecting their beliefs.

So relationship is one
of the most powerful tools for growth...
if we look honestly at our
relationships we can see so much
about how we
have created them.

SHAKTI GAWAIN
Creative Visualisation

There are
always risks
in freedom.

The only risk
in bondage
is that
of breaking free.

GITA BELLIN

Thoughts
are like
boomerangs.

EILEEN CADDY
The Dawn of Change

The most powerful thing
you can do to change the world,
is to change your own beliefs
about the nature of life, people,
reality, to something
more positive...
and begin to act
accordingly.

SHAKTI GAWAIN
Creative Visualisation

Be not the slave of your own past—
plunge into the sublime seas,
dive deep, and swim far,
so you shall come back
with self-respect,
with new power,
with an advanced experience,
that shall explain
and overlook
the old.

RALPH WALDO EMERSON

There is little sense in attempting
to change external conditions,
you must first change inner beliefs,
then outer conditions
will change accordingly.

BRIAN ADAMS
How To Succeed

The only way to deal
with the future
is to function efficiently
in the Now.

GITA BELLIN

All the world's a stage,
And all the men and women,
              merely players;
     They have their exits
              and their entrances,
And one man in his time
              plays many parts.

SHAKESPEARE
As You Like It

Stop sitting there
   with your hands folded
   looking on, doing nothing;

Get into action
   and live this full
        and glorious life.

Now.

You have to do it.

EILEEN CADDY
The Dawn of Change

Doubt is a pain
too lonely to know
that faith
is his twin brother.

KAHLIL GIBRAN
The Prophet

There is no separation
between us and God –
we are divine expressions
of the creative principle ...
there can be no real lack or scarcity;
there is nothing we have to try
to achieve or attract;
we contain the potential
for everything
within us.

SHAKTI GAWAIN
Creative Visualisation

See every difficulty
as a challenge,
a stepping stone,
and never be defeated
by anything
or anyone.

EILEEN CADDY
The Dawn of Change

*Success depends
on where intention
is.*

GITA BELLIN

If you shut your door
to all errors
truth will be
shut out.

RABINDRANATH TAGORE

Life is like a wild tiger.
You can either lie down
                and let it
Lay its paw on your head –
Or sit on its back and ride it.

RIDE THE WILD TIGER

Your subconscious mind has the answer.

If you are confronted with a problem
and you cannot see an immediate answer,
assume that your subconscious has the
solution and is waiting to reveal it to you.

If an answer does not come, turn the
problem over to your deeper mind
prior to sleep. Keep on turning your request
over to your subconscious until the
answer comes.

The response will be a certain 'feeling',
an inner awareness, whereby you
'know' what to do. Guidance in all things
comes as the still small voice within:
It reveals all.

BRIAN ADAMS
How To Succeed

Faith is an oasis
in the heart
which will never be reached
by the caravan of
thinking.

KAHLIL GIBRAN
Sand and Foam

Everytime we say
"I must do something"
it takes an incredible
amount of energy.

Far more
than physically
doing it.

GITA BELLIN

Be realistic:

Plan for a miracle.

BHAGWAN SHREE RAJNEESH

We are members
of a vast cosmic orchestra,
in which each living instrument
is essential to the
complementary and
harmonious
playing of
the
whole.

J. ALLEN BOONE
Kinship With All Life

Go confidently
in the direction of your dreams!
Live the life you've imagined.

As you simplify your life,
the laws of the universe
will be simpler;
solitude will not be solitude,
poverty will not be poverty,
nor weakness weakness.

HENRY DAVID THOREAU

What things soever ye desire,
when ye pray,
believe that ye receive them,
and ye shall have them.

MARK 11:24

Giving means extending one's
Love with no conditions, no
expectations and no boundaries.

Peace of mind occurs, therefore
when we put all our attention
into giving and have no desire
to get anything from, or to
change, another person.

The giving motivation leads
to a sense of inner peace and
joy that is unrelated to time.

GERALD G. JAMPOLSKY
Love is Letting Go of Fear

The only successful manifestation
is one which brings about a change
or growth in consciousness:
    that is, it has manifested God,
    or revealed him more fully,
    as well as having
        manifested a form...

DAVID SPANGLER
Manifestation

One may not
reach the dawn
save by
the path
of the night.

KAHLIL GIBRAN
Sand and Foam

We can only be here now
when we accept instantly
our moment-by-moment
emotional experience.

GITA BELLIN

We are not here just to survive
and live long...
We are here to live and know life
in its multi-dimensions
to know life in its richness,
in all its variety.

And when a man lives
multi-dimensionally,
explores all possibilities available,
never shrinks back from any challenge,
goes, rushes to it, welcomes it,
rises to the occasion
then life becomes a flame,
life blooms.

BHAGWAN SHREE RAJNEESH
The Sacred Yes

Your pain
is the breaking
of the shell
that encloses
your understanding.

KAHLIL GIBRAN
The Prophet

*You should always
be aware that your
head creates
your world.*

KEN KEYES, JR
Handbook to Higher Consciousness

Men are disturbed not by things
that happen,
but by their opinion of the things
that happen.

EPICTETUS

Gratitude
  helps you to grow and expand;
  gratitude brings joy
  and laughter into your lives
  and into the lives of all those
              around you.

EILEEN CADDY
The Dawn of Change

You are never asked
to do more than you are able
without being given
the strength and ability
to do it.

EILEEN CADDY
The Dawn of Change

*If one desires a change,
one must be that change
before that change
can take place.*

GITA BELLIN

A changed thought system can reverse cause-and-effect as we have known it. For most of us, this is a very difficult concept to accept, because of our resistance to relinquishing the predictability of our past belief system and to assuming responsibility for our thoughts, feelings and reactions.

Since we always look within before looking out, we can perceive attack outside us only when we have first accepted attack as real within.

GERALD G. JAMPOLSKY
Love is Letting Go of Fear

Be outrageous !

People who
achieve mastery
have the ability
to be outrageous.

GITA BELLIN

The divinest things - religion, love,
truth, beauty, justice - seem to lose
their meaning and value when we
sink into lassitude and indifference...
    It is a signal that we should quit
meditation and books and go out into
the open air, into the presence of
nature, into the company of flocks
and children, where we may drink
new health and vigour from the
clear and full-flowing fountains
of life, afar from the arid wastes
of theory and speculation; where
we may learn again that it is not
by intellectual questionings, but by
believing, hoping, loving, and doing
that man finds joy and peace.

JOHN LANCASTER SPALDING

Expect the best;
    convert problems into opportunities;
Be dissatisfied with the status quo;
    Focus on where you want to go,
        instead of where you're coming from;
and most importantly,
    Decide to be happy,
        Knowing it's an attitude,
           a habit gained from daily practice,
            and not a result or payoff.

DENIS WAITLEY
The Winner's Edge

Everyone
and everything
around you
is your
teacher.

KEN KEYES, JR
Handbook to Higher Consciousness

Peace of mind
comes from not wanting
to change others,
but by simply accepting them
as they are.

True acceptance
is always without demands
and expectations.

GERALD G. JAMPOLSKY
Love is Letting Go of Fear

To hate another is to hate yourself.
We all live within the one Universal Mind.
What we think about another,
we think about ourselves.

If you have an enemy, forgive him now.
Let all bitterness and resentment dissolve.
You owe your fellow man love;
show him love, not hate.

Show charity and goodwill toward others
and it will return to enhance
your own life
in many wonderful ways.

BRIAN ADAMS
How To Succeed

Disillusionment
with yourself
must precede
Enlightenment.

VERNON HOWARD
The Mystic Path to Cosmic Power

Love
   is a space
      in which
      all other emotions
   can be experienced.

ROBERT PRINABLE

Before enlightenment
  chopping wood
  carrying water.

After enlightenment
  chopping wood
  carrying water.

ZEN PROVERB

The measure of mental health
is the disposition to find good
everywhere.

RALPH WALDO EMERSON

Truth does not change
although
    your perception of it
may vary
or alter
        drastically.

JOHN & LYN ST·CLAIR THOMAS
Eyes of the Beholder

Learn your lessons
quickly,

and move on.

EILEEN CADDY
The Dawn of Change

Life has its sleep, its periods of inactivity, when it loses its movements, takes no new food, living upon its past storage. Then it grows helpless, its muscles relaxed, and it easily lends itself to be jeered at for its stupour.

In the rhythm of life, pauses there must be for the renewal of life. Life in its activity is ever spending itself, burning all its fuel.

This extravagance cannot go on indefinitely, but is always followed by a passive stage, when all expenditure is stopped and all adventures abandoned in favour of rest and slow recuperation.

RABINDRANATH TAGORE

People with high self esteem have it
    because they have overcome their failures.

They have been put to the test of life,
    overcome the problems
            and grown.

DAVID JANSEN

The fastest way
to freedom
is to
feel
your feelings.

GITA BELLIN

Do not take life's experiences
too seriously. Above all, do not
let them hurt you, for in reality
they are nothing but
dream experiences....

If circumstances are bad
and you have to bear them,
do not make them
a part of yourself.

Play your part in life,
but never forget that
it is only a role.

PARAMAHANSA YOGANANDA
Par-a-gram

The snow goose
 need not bathe
   to make itself white.

Neither need you
  do anything
    but be yourself.

LAO-TSE

Be like a very small
joyous child
living gloriously in the
ever present Now
without a single worry or concern
about even the next
moment of time.

EILEEN CADDY
The Dawn of Change

There is but one cause
of human failure
and that is
man's lack of faith
in his true Self.

WILLIAM JAMES

We are injured and hurt emotionally
- not so much by other people
or what they say or don't say -
but by our own attitude
and our own response.

MAXWELL MALTZ
Psycho-Cybernetics

Until
    you can understand
      that nothing can happen to you,
    nothing can ever come to you
  or be kept from you,
except in accord
  with your state
    of consciousness,
      you do not have
        the key to life.

PAUL TWITCHELL
The Flute of God
ECKANKAR

If you depend on someone
 for your happiness
  you are becoming a slave,
   you are becoming dependent,
    you are creating a bondage.

  And you depend on
   so many people; they all
  become subtle masters,
 they all exploit you in return.

BHAGWAN SHREE RAJNEESH
The Book of the Books Vol. IV

Be not heedful of the morrow,
but rather gaze upon today,
for sufficient for today
is the miracle thereof.

Be not overmindful
of yourself when you give
but be mindful of the necessity.
For every giver himself receives from
the Father, and that much more
abundantly.

ANNIE BESANT
Some Difficulties of the Inner Life

Life's fulfillment finds constant contradictions in its path; but those are necessary for the sake of its advance.

The stream is saved from the sluggishness of its current by the perpetual opposition of the soil through which it must cut its way. It is the soil which forms its banks.

The Spirit of fight belongs to the genius of life.

RABINDRANATH TAGORE

Take heart,
    truth and happiness
        will get you in the end.

You can't lose in this game.

Have fun.

It goes on too long
    to be taken seriously
        all the time.

JOHN & LYN ST. CLAIR THOMAS
Eyes of the Beholder

How wonderful is the way in which, with quite ordinary folk, power leaps to our aid in any time of emergency. We lead timid lives, shrinking from difficult tasks till perhaps we are forced into them or ourselves determine on them, and immediately we seem to unlock the unseen forces. When we have to face danger, then courage comes, when trial puts a long-continued strain upon us, we find ourselves possessed by the power to endure; if when disaster ultimately brings the fall which we so long dreaded, we feel underneath us the strength as of the everlasting arms. Common experience teaches that, when great demands are made upon us, if only we fearlessly accept the challenge and confidently expend our strength, every danger or difficulty brings its own strength - "As thy days so shall thy strength be."

J. A. HADFIELD
The Psychology of Power

Work
is love
made visible.

KAHLIL GIBRAN
The Prophet

All things are in the act of change:
thou thyself in ceaseless transformation
and partial decay,
and the whole universe
with thee.

MARCUS AURELIUS ANTONIUS

Man has falsely identified
  himself with the pseudo-soul
  or ego.
When he transfers his sense
  of identity to his true being,
  the immortal Soul,
  he discovers that
  all pain is unreal.
    He no longer
      can even imagine
      the state of suffering.

PARAMAHANSA YOGANANDA
Sayings of Paramahansa Yogananda

How soon
  will you realise
  that the only thing
  you don't have is
  the direct experience

    that there's
    nothing you need

  that you
  don't have ?

KEN KEYES, JR
Handbook to Higher Consciousness

Regrets
can hold you back
and can prevent the most
wonderful things
taking place
in your
lives.

EILEEN CADDY
Footprints on the Path

You will have
    wonderful surges forward.
Then there must be
    a time of consolidating
    before the next forward surge.

    Accept this
        as part of the process
        and never become
            downhearted.

EILEEN CADDY
God Spoke to Me

Don't try to force anything.
Let life be a deep let-go.

See God opening millions
of flowers every day
without forcing
the buds.

BHAGWAN SHREE RAJNEESH
Dying for Enlightenment

Come to the edge, he said.
They said: We are afraid.
Come to the edge, he said.
They came.
He pushed them...and they flew.

GUILLAUME APOLLINAIRE

Do not be desirous of having
things done quickly. Do not
look at small advantages.
Desire to have things done
quickly prevents their being
done thoroughly. Looking
at small advantages prevents
great affairs from being
accomplished.

CONFUCIUS

... as the springs return -
regardless of time or man -
so is HOPE !
Sometimes but a tiny bud
that has to push up
through the hard shell
of circumstance
to reach the light
of accomplishment.
Do not give up HOPE !

DOROTHY MILLER COLE

You must begin
to trust yourself.

If you do not
then you will forever
be looking to others
to prove your own merit to you,
and you will never be satisfied.

You will always be asking
others what to do,
and at the same time
resenting those
from whom
you seek such aid.

JANE ROBERTS
The Nature of Personal Reality

You know quite well,
deep within you,
that there is only
a single magic,
a single power,
a single salvation...
and that is called loving.
Well then,
love your suffering.
Do not resist it, do not flee from it
It is only your aversion that hurts,
nothing else.

HERMAN HESSE

'When one realises
    one is asleep,
    at that moment
      one is already half-awake.

P.D. OUSPENSKY &
G.I. GURDJIEFF

We are built to conquer environment,
solve problems, achieve goals,
and we find no real satisfaction
or happiness in life
without obstacles to conquer
and goals to achieve.

MAXWELL MALTZ
Psycho-Cybernetics

Most people don't know
how brave they really are.

In fact, many potential heroes,
both men and women,
live out their lives in self-doubt.

If they only knew they had
these deep resources,
it would help give them the self-reliance
to meet most problems,
even a big crisis.

R.E. CHAMBERS

Realise that you cannot
help a soul unless that soul
really wants help and is
ready to be helped.

I tell you to send that soul
nothing but Love and more Love.

Be still and wait,
but be there when that soul
turns for help.

EILEEN CADDY
God Spoke to Me

No soul that aspires
can ever fail to rise ;
no heart that loves
can ever be abandoned.

Difficulties exist only
that in overcoming them
we may grow strong,
and they only who
who have suffered
are able to save.

ANNIE BESANT
Some Difficulties of the Inner Life

Be aware of the reality of your feelings. As you become more aware of your beliefs over a period of time, you will see how they bring forth certain feelings automatically.

A man who is sure of himself is _not_ angry at every slight done him, nor does he carry grudges. A man who fears for his own worth, however, _is_ furious under such conditions.

The free flow of your emotions will always lead you back to your conscious beliefs if you do not impede them.

JANE ROBERTS
The Nature of Personal Reality

'Begin with the possible;
begin with one step.
There is always a limit,
you cannot do more than you can.
If you try to do too much,
you will do nothing.

P. D. OUSPENSKY &
G. I. GURDJIEFF

You must love yourself
before you love another.

By accepting yourself
and joyfully
being what you are,
you fulfill your own abilities,
and your simple presence
can make
others happy.

JANE ROBERTS
The Nature of Personal Reality

Ideas by themselves
cannot produce change of being;
your effort must go in the
right direction,
and one must correspond
to the other.

P. D. OUSPENSKY
G. I. GURDJIEFF

There is much to use of nature's way.
It is with you always,
  available to you always.

    Take time to hear and see
    that which is close at hand.

There are forces in you untried.

They are yours to be used
  as you find them.

JOHN & LYN ST. CLAIR-THOMAS
Eyes of the Beholder

You will decide
on a matter,
and it will be
established for you,
and light will shine
on your ways.

JOB 22:28

A loving
   person lives
      in
a loving world

A hostile
   person lives
      in
a hostile world.

Everyone you meet
is your mirror.

KEN KEYES, JR
Handbook to Higher Consciousness

All the powers of your inner Self are set into activation as a result of your conscious beliefs. You have lost a sense of responsibility for your conscious thought because you have been taught that it is not what forms your life. You have been told that regardless of your belief you are terrorized by unconscious conditioning.

Some of your beliefs originated in your childhood, but you are not at their mercy unless you _believe_ that you are.

JANE ROBERTS
The Nature of Personal Reality

Each player must accept the cards
   life deals him or her.

But once they are in hand,
   he or she alone must decide
      how to play the cards
         in order to win the game.

VOLTAIRE

A person who is not disturbed
by the incessant flow of desires-
that enter like rivers into the
ocean, which is ever being
filled but is always still -
can alone achieve peace,
and not the man who strives
to satisfy such desires.

BHAGAVAD-GITA II:70

Stop looking
      for a scapegoat
         in your life
but be willing
   to face the truth
      within yourself
         and right
            your own wrongs.

EILEEN CADDY
Footprints on the Path

It is important
from time to time
to slow down,
to go away by yourself,
and simply
Be.

EILEEN CADDY
The Dawn of Change

Life has a bright side and a dark side,
 for the world of relativity
 is composed of light and shadows.

If you permit your thoughts
 to dwell on evil,
 you yourself will become ugly.

Look only for the good
 in everything,
 that you absorb
 the quality of beauty.

PARAMAHANSA YOGANANDA
Sayings of Paramahansa Yogananda

What is of all things most yielding
Can overcome that which is most hard
Being substanceless, it can enter in
even where there is no crevice.
That is how I know the value of
action which is actionless.
But that there can be teaching
without words
Value in action which is actionless
Few indeed can understand.
That the yielding conquers the resistant
and the soft conquers the hard
is a fact known by all
but utilized by none.

LAO TZU

*I know I'm not seeing things
as they are,*

I'm seeing things as I am.

LAUREL LEE

Be very very still
    and allow every new experience
    to take place in your life
    without any resistance
        whatsoever.

You do not have to do anything,
    you simply have to be
    and let things happen.

EILEEN CADDY
Footprints on the Path

Not judging is another way
of letting go of fear and experiencing
Love.

When we learn not to judge
others - and totally accept them,
and not want to change them -
we can simultaneously learn to
accept ourselves.

GERALD G. JAMPOLSKY
Love is Letting Go of Fear

The difference between
a flower and a weed
is a judgement.

A man must elevate himself
by his own mind,
not degrade himself.

The mind is the friend
of the conditioned soul,
and his enemy as well.

BHAGAVAD-GITA VI:5

*Every end
is a new
beginning.*

Acknowledgements

Especially I wish to thank Malcolm Cohan for his love, and constant encouragement without which this book would have never been started, sustained or completed.

I would like to thank Margo Snape for her beautiful artwork for the cover; and to Shane McCoy for his wonderful illustrations.

Further, I would like to express my deepest thanks to my family and friends whose presence in my life contributed, whether directly or indirectly, towards the book.

Finally, I would like to acknowledge all the great spirits I have quoted in this book whose words have given so much to my understanding and growth.

I am grateful to the publishers who kindly gave me permission to reproduce copyright material. These quotations were extracted from the following publications:

BRIAN ADAMS, *How To Succeed*, Copyright © 1985 by Brian Adams. Published by Melvin Powers Wilshire Book Company, California, USA.

GITA BELLIN & THE SELF-TRANSFORMATION CENTRE, *A Sharing of Completion*, Copyright © 1983 Self-Transformation Seminars Ltd.

J. ALLEN BOONE, *Kinship With All Life*, Copyright © 1954 by Harper & Row, Publishers, Inc., New York. By permission of the Publisher.

ASHLEIGH BRILLIANT, *I Have Abandoned My Search For Truth And Am Now Looking For A Good Fantasy*, Copyright © 1980 Ashleigh Brilliant, Woodbridge Press, California.

EILEEN CADDY, *The Dawn of Change*, Copyright © 1979 The Findhorn Press, *God Spoke To Me*, Copyright © 1971 The Findhorn Press, *Footprints On The Path*, Copyright © 1976 Eileen Caddy.